BEYOND CANDY YAMS & SWEET POTATO PIE

BOOK FOR COOKING FABULOUSLY HEALTHY AND DELICIOUS FOODS

Velonda Thompson, Ph.D.

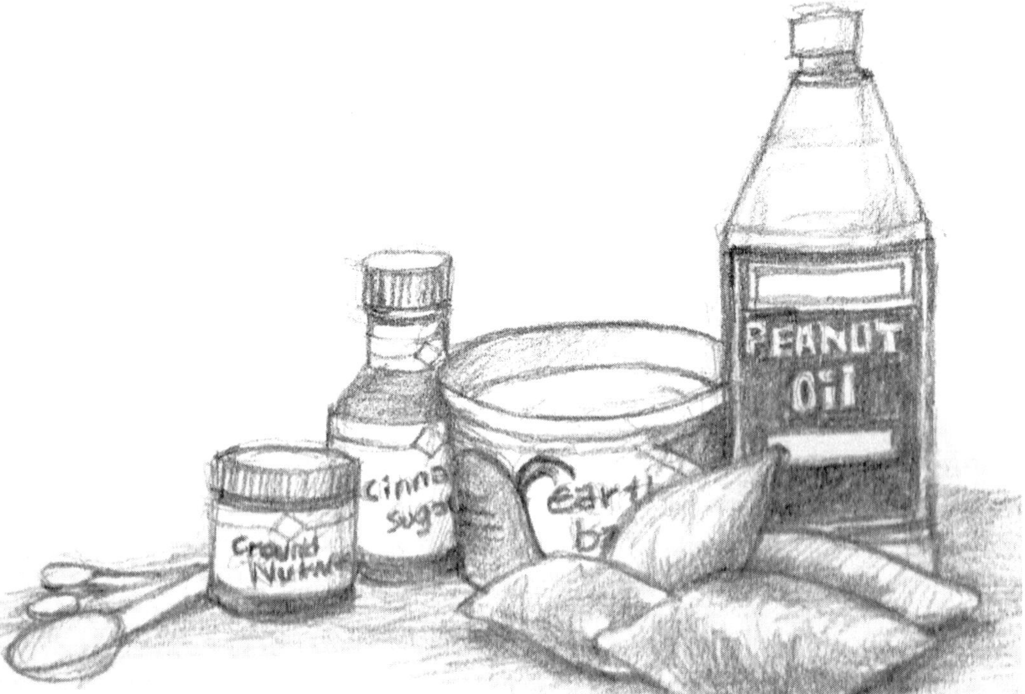
PEANUT
Oil
Ground

BEYOND CANDY YAMS & SWEET POTATO PIE

Velonda Thompson, Ph.D.

My Vision Works Publishing
Farmington Hills, Michigan

Published by My Vision Works Publishing
30777 Northwestern Hwy, Suite 110
Farmington Hills, MI 48334

Copyright © 2011 Be-Fit, Inc.
Reprinted, 2013

All rights reserved.

Written permission must be secured from the author to use or reproduce any part of this work, except for brief quotations in critical reviews or articles.

Library of Congress Cataloging-In-Publication Data

Printed in the United States
ISBN: 9781468053432

"Let your food be your medicine and your medicine be your food."

~ Hippocrates

CONTENTS

Acknowledgments V

Entrees & Sides 1

Soups & Salads 36

How Sweet It Is 55

Sweets & Treat 63

Cooking with Tempeh 83

Awesome Rawsome 98

Plant-based eating made easy 103

Afterword 106

Endnotes 107

Index 108

About the author 112

DEDICATION

This book is dedicated to the gardeners, foodies, wholistic practitioners and many nutrition and health education mentors who have coached me and cajoled me on my sweet potato journey. To the many students, clients, and unsuspecting teachers, I offer humble gratitude.

ACKNOWLEDGEMENTS

I trust that I have given adequate credit throughout the pages of this book to those on whose expertise upon which I have relied.

And finally to the many individuals who have lent their taste buds to my creations, read my books and attended my Tasteshops[sm]. Without you this publication would not be possible.

Velonda Thompson, PhD
Detroit, Michigan 2013

FOREWORD

In the last several years, there has been great interest in Mediterranean style and plant focused diets. Most offerings in this area are soy-based which can present some dietary difficulties. This book is an addition to the critical movement toward plant-focused eating; while, for the most part, avoiding the difficulties that can be encountered with soy. Dr. Thompson has followed up her previous book, *Pass the Sweet Potatoes, Please* with more recipes and even more useful supporting information.

Almost every restaurant has some version or offering of a sweet potato recipe. Those menus don't inform the reader about the health benefits of this newly rediscovered food. There is much in the current literature about the advantages of consuming carotenoids. Some people take their carotenoids as pills or capsules. I urge you to consume yours as sweet potatoes, using the delightful and easy to prepare recipes found in this book.

My commitments require a lot of time and for this reason, I generally do not have much time review cookbooks. However, because of the wealth of useful and important information, this was important. Dr. Thompson's comments are concise and the information is priceless.

H. Ira Fritz Ph.D., CNS, FACN

Impomoea Batatas is its botanical name.

Tasty roots – its reason for fame.

A dependable yield under adverse condition.

Many survived due to its superior nutrition [1]

INTRODUCING SWEET *Potatoes*

They come in the "Jewel" and "Centennial" variety. The sweet potato has been an important crop in this country since the 18th century, believed to have arrived from South America gaining worldwide distribution between the 15-17th centuries. [2]

When George Washington Carver arrived at Tuskegee Institute in the fall of 1896 to direct the newly organized department of agriculture, the south was very dependent on cotton. Cotton, however, had depleted the soil and threatened the region's economy. Carver provided some relief for the farmers by developing not only the peanut and soybean, but also the sweet potato. He ultimately developed over 125 products from the sweet potato, including flour, vinegar, molasses, rubber, ink and postage stamp glue. Although George Washington Carver died in 1943, extensive sweet potato research has continued at Tuskegee as well as the development and distribution of a variety of frozen sweet potato products.

Knowing what I know about sweet potatoes ,also known as yams, the nutritionist in me ponders why we feel the need to candy an already sweet and incredibly palate stimulating vegetable as this wonder potato. Yes, we hippies, yuppies and buppies grew up on mama's candied yams and grandma's sweet potato pie.

A recent Google image search using the keyword "sweet potato" yielded 5,560,000 images. With that many images, it goes without saying that there are a lot of sweet potato lovers. For those that wish to cook it's impossible not to explore *"Beyond Candies Yams and Sweet Potato Pie*

1

ENTREES AND SIDES

Change your diet to change your destiny!

ENTREES & SIDES

A nibble on the run or the main act of the meal, makes these recipes 5-star options, morning, noon or night.

You say potato, I say SWEET!

STOVE TOP ROASTED SWEET POTATOES

4 small Sweet potatoes
2 tablespoons peanut Oil
Cinnamon sugar
Nutmeg
Vegetarian margarine (Earth Balance)

1. Parboil sweet potatoes, but do not peel. Cut the potatoes into medium cubes.
2. Coat frying pan (cast iron preferred) with peanut oil then generously sprinkle cinnamon sugar & nutmeg on top of oil.
3. Layer cubed sweet potatoes and top with soft margarine, nutmeg & cinnamon sugar.
4. Cover & cook low-medium heat until tender.

BROCCOLI PORTABELLA BAKE WITH A SWEET POTATO CRUST

¼ teaspoon pumpkin pie spice
3 cups sweet potatoes, cooked and mashed
2 tablespoons vegetarian margarine, melted
2 cups portabella mushrooms, cubed
1 10-ounce can low-fat, low-sodium cream of celery soup
1 cup broccoli, chopped
1 tablespoon black pepper
nonstick cooking spray

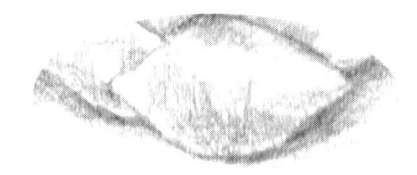

1. Preheat oven to 350F
2. Combine pumpkin pie spice, sweet potatoes and margarine in a medium bowl. Blend until smooth.
3. Spray 9-inch pie pan with non-stick cooking spray
4. Line pan with potato mixture to form a pie shell. Set aside.
5. Combine mushrooms, soup, broccoli and pepper in a medium bowl.
6. Pour mushroom mixture into prepared pie pan.
7. Bake for approximately 1 hour

What Americans call yams are actually one of many varieties of sweet potatoes. The American yam is the moist, sweet, orange skinned type of sweet potato; which were renamed yams in an effort to tell them apart from their sweet potato cousins who are lighter and less sweet. Yams actually come from Africa and sweet potatoes are native to Central America. The inner flesh of the sweet potato is brimming with beta-carotene along with vitamin c, fiber, potassium, iron, and manganese. The outer skin is where you will find three times the amount of anti-oxidants as their inner flesh.

Roasted Rosemary Sweet Potato Wedges

ROASTED ROSEMARY SWEET POTATO WEDGES

6 medium sweet potatoes
3 tablespoons sesame seed oil
1 teaspoon chili powder
1 tablespoon Bragg Liquid Aminos (or low sodium soy-sauce)
1 tablespoon ground rosemary

Preheat oven to 450F

1. Halve potatoes crosswise, then length-wise and cut into sticks and place in a large mixing bowl. Mix oil, chili powder and soy sauce together then pour over potatoes.
2. Toss potatoes in oil mixture to thoroughly coat. Place potatoes, skin side down in non-stick roasting pan. Roast 10 – 12 minutes then turn slices and roast until tender.
3. **Sprinkle with rosemary and serve.**

SWEET POTATO PANCAKES

1 cup oat flour
2 teaspoons baking powder (aluminum free)
½ teaspoon sea salt
¼ teaspoon ground nutmeg
1 cup mashed cooked sweet potatoes
¼ cup egg substitute
1 cup almond milk
1 tablespoon vegan butter

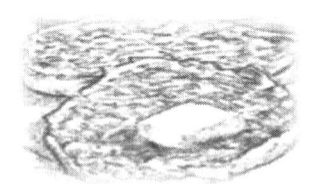

1. In a medium bowl, whisk together dry ingredients
2. Mix mashed sweet potatoes, eggs, milk and butter in a separate medium bowl.
3. Blend sweet potato mixture into the flour mixture to form a batter.
4. Preheat a lightly greased griddle over medium-high heat.
5. Drop 1/3 cup batter mixture onto hot oiled skillet or griddle for each pancake Cook until golden brown, turning once.
6. Great with maple syrup or cranberry sauce

VEGETABLE SWEET POTATO PANCAKES

1 medium sweet potato, grated
1 medium idaho potato, grated
1 medium onion, grated
1 small zucchini, grated
1 tablespoon basil
¼ cup egg substitute
3 tablespoons whole wheat flour (or unbleached white flour)
Pepper to taste
1 tablespoon peanut oil

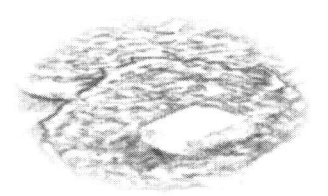

1. In a large bowl, mix all ingredients together
2. Add more flour if necessary
3. Spoon ¼ cup batter for each pancake. Sauté in oil.
4. Turn when brown on one side and sauté on the other side
5. Serve immediately

With their dark-amber skin and bright-orange filling, sweet potatoes are a great source of beta-carotene, fiber, and vitamins B6 and C. Using them in your healthy kitchen is a no-brainer as well. You can substitute sweet potatoes for any dish that calls for white potatoes. Sweet potatoes are available sporadically year-round, but they're at their sweetest in fall and winter.

SWEET POTATO BISCUITS

SWEET POTATO BISCUITS

2 cups sweet potatoes, cooked and mashed
¼ cup vegan butter
½ cups almond milk
1 tablespoon maple syrup
2 cup oat flour
2 teaspoon baking powder
½ teaspoon sea salt
1/8 teaspoon ground nutmeg

1. Preheat oven to 450F
2. Mix together potatoes and butter. Add milk and maple syrup. In a separate bowl, sift together flour, baking powder, sea salt and nutmeg.
3. Form a soft dough by combining the sweet potato mixture and the flour mixture. On a floured sheet/board turn dough while kneading until the outside looks smooth.
4. Roll dough out to a ½ - inch thickness and cut biscuits. Reroll scraps and cut biscuits until all dough is used. Place biscuits on a baking sheet, ½ inch apart and bake until golden brown.

YAM DIP

1 pint plain nonfat yogurt
1 package onion soup mix
½ cup mashed sweet potatoes

1. Mix ingredients together and chill
2. Serve with fresh vegetables

Source: The Louisiana Sweet Potato Commission

Agricultural Research scientist William Walter (1988) once said "French frying the sweet potato may liberate that root vegetable from its traditional place at the holiday table and put it on restaurant menus right alongside the more popular white potato". While I'm not so sure of how much liberation the sweet potato has enjoyed, I can see sweet potato fries can be found on many restaurant menus across the globe.

SWEET POTATO FRIES

2 large sweet potatoes
2 tablespoons peanut oil
Seasoned salt
Cinnamon

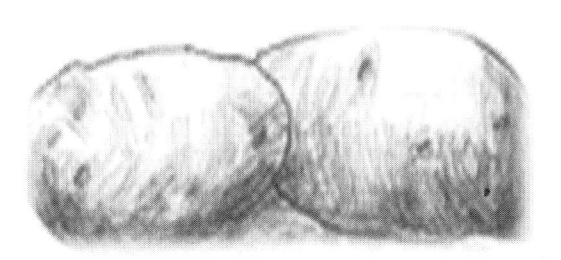

1. Preheat oven to 350F
2. Cut sweet potatoes into strips ¼ inch thick and ¼ inch wide
3. Prepare baking sheet with 1 tablespoon peanut oil
4. Toss potato strips in 1 tablespoon peanut oil
5. Spread potato strips on baking sheet in one layer
6. Sprinkle with seasoned salt
7. Sprinkle with cinnamon
8. Bake for approximately 30 minutes or until thoroughly cooked

The sweet potato is a fleshy root originating in South and Central America. By the time Columbus came to America in 1492, many varieties were already being grown. This new food was probably bought to Europe about 1500 from the West Indies. Between late 1800's and early 1900's, over 100 sweet potato products were developed and patented by George Washington Carver.

SWEET POTATO CRAB CAKE

SWEET POTATO CRAB CAKE

1 pound crab meat
1 cup mashed sweet potato
1 cup bread crumbs
1/3 cup chopped red onions
½ cup egg substitute
Peanut oil

1. Combine crabmeat, sweet potato, ½ cup bread crumbs, onions and egg substitute
2. Form into medium patties
3. Coat patties with remaining bread crumbs
4. Cook over medium heat until golden brown on each side

Sweet Potato Quiche

SWEET POTATO QUICHE

1 cup mashed sweet potato
¼ cup green pepper, chopped
¼ cup shallot, chopped
1 tablespoon minced garlic
1 cup Eggbeaters
1 cup chopped eggplant
½ cup low-fat Italian blend cheese
1 cup chopped portabella mushroom
¼ cup red pepper
¼ cup orange pepper

1. Mix sweet potato, pepper, shallot, garlic and eggbeater together
2. Fold in eggplant
3. Pour the filling carefully into the prepared pie dish or 9 inch square baking dish.
4. Top with cheese
5. Bake at 375°F for 40 minutes or until the filling is firm.

Many professional athletes consider sweet potatoes to be one of the top high-energy foods. This is because the average sweet potato is low in cholesterol and sodium, virtually fat free and loaded with fiber. Sweet potatoes are an excellent source of pro-vitamin A (carotene) which is converted into vitamin A (retinol) by the body (Collins and Walter, 1982).

SWEET POTATO ZUCCHINI BAKE

2 cups grated zucchini
1 teaspoon sea salt
1 cup organic whole wheat flour
½ teaspoon baking powder
½ tablespoon fresh thyme leaves
½ tablespoon ground black pepper
½ cup onion, diced
1 cup grated cheese
½ cup safflower oil
½ cup eggbeaters
½ cup mashed sweet potato
¼ teaspoon vegan margarine

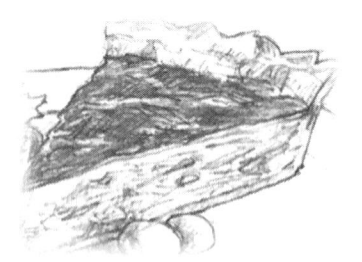

1. Preheat oven to 350F
2. Grease baking dish with margarine
3. Combine zucchini and sea salt in a colander. Set aside to drain
4. In medium bowl stir together flour, baking powder, thyme and pepper.
5. Add onion, zucchini and cheese to flour mixture. Mix well, breaking up any clumps.
6. Whisk together oil and eggbeaters. Pour into zucchini mixture and mix well.
7. Add sweet potato to zucchini mixture and mix well.
8. Pour into prepared baking dish
9. Bake for 40 – 45 minutes
10. Cool for approximate 10 minutes. Cut into squares and serve.

Sweet Potatoes and Greens

SWEET POTATOES AND GREENS

1 pound fresh collard greens, trimmed & chopped
3 large sweet potatoes
2 tablespoon   safflower oil
1 cup water
2 cloves of garlic, chopped fine
1 teaspoon agave nectar
½ teaspoon lemon juice
½ teaspoon cinnamon
Ground black pepper

1. Heat the oil in large skillet over medium heat, add garlic and cook for 1 minute. Add greens, stirring to thoroughly coat. Add water, simmer for 10 minutes, stirring occasionally.
2. While the greens are cooking, peel and cut the sweet potatoes into bite size cubes. After simmering for ten minutes, add sweet potatoes and cinnamon to the skillet.
3. Cook, stirring occasionally, until potatoes and greens are tender.
4. Season with pepper to taste.
5. Combine agave nectar and lemon juice and add to potatoes and greens, stir and serve.

SWEET POTATO & RED PEPPER PASTA

8 ounces whole-wheat angel hair pasta
2 tablespoons extra-virgin olive oil, divided
4 cloves garlic, minced
1 medium sweet potato, peeled and shredded
1 large red bell pepper, thinly sliced
1 cup diced plum tomatoes
1/2 cup water
2 tablespoons chopped fresh parsley
1 tablespoon basil
1 tablespoon lemon juice
3/4 teaspoon sea salt
1/2 cup crumbled goat cheese

1. In a large pot cook pasta until tender, 4-5 minutes or according to package directions. Drain pasta, reserving 1/2 cup of cooking water. Return pasta to pot and set aside.

2. Place 1 tablespoon oil and garlic in a large skillet. Cook over medium heat, stirring occasionally, until garlic is sizzling and fragrant, 2-5 minutes. Add sweet potato, bell pepper, tomatoes and water and cook, approximately 5-7 minutes, until bell pepper is tender-crisp, stirring occasionally, Remove from heat; cover and keep warm.

3. Add vegetable mixture to pasta, remaining 1 tablespoon oil, parsley, basil, oregano, lemon juice, salt and cheese; toss to combine. Add reserved pasta water, 2 tablespoons at a time, to achieve desired consistency.

In addition to being a great source of complex carbohydrates, sweet potatoes are an important source of vitamin B6. Sweet potatoes contain the calcium and potassium, the minerals that your body needs to regulate heartbeat, blood pressure, and transmission of nerve impulses. They also contain significant amounts of folate.

A ½ cup of cooked sweet potatoes provides approximately 25 micrograms of folate, which is about 14% of the recommended daily allowance. According to Albert Purcell (1971), an 8-ounce sweet potato provides nearly 1/5 of the minimum daily protein needs and a 2 ½ day supply of iron for women.

Scalloped Potatoes

SCALLOPED POTATOES

2 cups sweet potatoes, peeled, cut into ¼-inch slices
4 cups russet potatoes, peeled, cut into ¼-inch slices
1 tablespoon sweet onion, finely chopped
½ teaspoon dried thyme
2 vegetable bouillon cubes
1 ½ cup almond milk
½ cup parmesan cheese

1. Heat milk, bouillon cubes and thyme in large skillet over medium high heat, stirring occasionally until bouillon is dissolved.
2. Add potatoes and cook until mixture comes to boil, stirring occasionally.
3. Reduce heat to low, cover and cook gently rearranging potatoes occasionally until potatoes are tender (approximately 35 minutes). Sprinkle with cheese and serve.

GRILLED SWEET POTATOES

4 medium sweet potatoes cut into 1 inch thick wedges
3 tablespoons Bragg Liquid Amino
2 tablespoon agave nectar (or sorghum molasses)
1 cup water
1 garlic clove, minced
1 tablespoon sesame oil

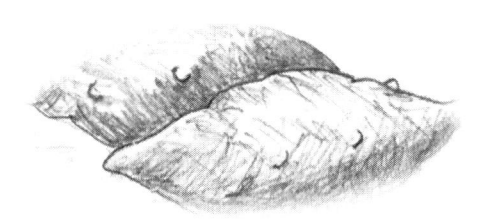

1. Combine Bragg, agave nectar, garlic, water in large bowl.
2. Add sweet potatoes and toss.
3. Drain and set marinade aside.
4. Arrange potato wedges in a grill basket.
5. Brush wedges with sesame oil.
6. Cover with a grill lid and cook for 15 minutes over medium coals, occasionally basting with remaining marinade.
7. Serve warm.

BROWN RICE VEGGIE CASSEROLE

1 1/2 cups cooked brown rice
1/2 cup broccoli florets
1/2 cup diced butternut squash
1 small carrot-grated
2 small portabella mushrooms-chopped
2 small white button mushrooms-chopped
1 tbsp Braggs Liquid Amino

1. Combine all ingredients and place in a casserole dish
2. Pour 1/3 cup water over mixture.
3. Cover and bake at 350 degrees for approximately 25 minutes.

BROWN RICE STUFFING

2 cups cooked brown rice
1 small onion, chopped (1/2 cup)
½ cup currants
1 small apple, cored & chopped
½ teaspoon each chopped basil
½ teaspoon each celery seeds
1 teaspoon cayenne pepper
2 tablespoon sesame oil

1. Combine all ingredients in large sauté pan.
2. Sauté, stirring frequently for approximately 10 minutes and Serve ;~)
3. The mixture can be stuffed in any squash and bake at 350° until tender.

Adapted from Raziyah Curtis's Stuffed Acorn Squash Recipe

A sweet potato is not a yam. Yams and sweet potatoes are both grown underground; however, this is where the similarities end. The sweet potato, which is commercially grown in the United States, is a fleshy non-tuberous root member of the genus ipomoea batatas family. It comes in two varieties. The most commonly seen variety has dark skin and deep orange flesh. The other variety has a light skin and beige or ivory flesh. The darker variety is sweet and most often mistaken for a yam. The yam is a large, starchy, tuberous root belonging to the genus ioscoea family.

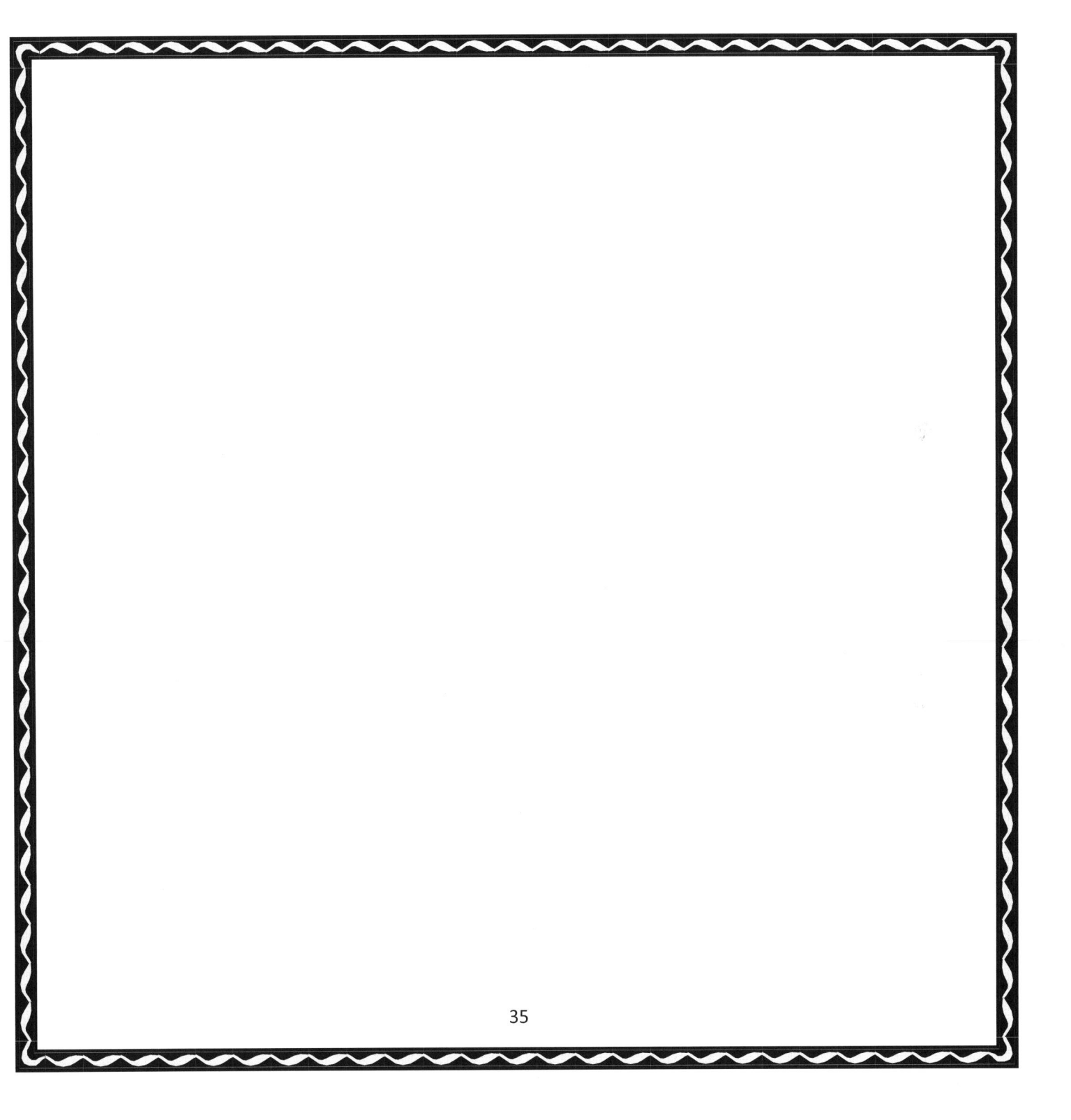

2

SOUPS AND SALADS

Leave your drugs in the chemist's pot if you can cure the patient with food.

~HIPPOCRATES

SOUPS & SALADS

You only need to add a robust bread in the winter or a light cracker in the spring to savor the flavor of these soups and salads.

The Louisiana Sweet Potato Commission calls the sweet potato the virtuous vegetable; one medium sweet potato provides over 1/3 of our daily vitamin C requirements. According to the North Carolina Sweet Potato Commission, it would take 23 cups of broccoli to equal the same amount of beta-carotene as one medium sweet potato.

CHERRY-TATER SALAD

2 pounds sweet potatoes, cooked, peeled and cut into bite sized cubes
½ cup ground cherries, halved
½ cup dried cranberries
¼ cup raisins
¼ cup chopped walnuts
½ cup Grapeseed Vegenaise*
1 tablespoon lemon juice
1 tablespoon orange juice
1 teaspoon grated orange peel
½ teaspoon grated ginger
¼ teaspoon nutmeg

1. In large bowl, combine, potatoes, ground cherries, cranberries, raisins and walnuts.
2. In small bowl, combine vegennaise, lemon juice, orange juice, orange peel, ginger and nutmeg.
3. Fold juice mixture into potato mixture.
4. Cover and chill for 2 hours.

Grapeseed Veganaise is an egg free, gluten free salad dressing and sandwich spread manufactured by Earth Island®
Dedicated to the Garden Resource Program in Detroit, MI

Sweet Potato Chili

SWEET POTATO CHILI

2 teaspoon extra virgin olive oil
1 small onion, diced
1 small sweet potato, diced
2 cloves garlic, minced
1 Tablespoon chili powder (to taste)
2 teaspoon cumin
4 ozs. green chilies (canned)
1/8 teaspoono salt
1 1/3 cup low sodium tomato juice
1 can black beans, rinsed (15 ozs.)
1 cup diced tomatoes (canned)
2 Tbsp. fresh cilantro, chopped fine

1. Add onion and potato, stirring often, cook for about 5 minutes until onion and potato begin to soften.
2. Add garlic, chili powder, cumin, chipotle chili and salt. Stir constantly for about a minute.
3. Add tomato juice and bring to a light boil. Reduce heat to simmer.
4. Cover and cook about 10-12 minutes until potato is fork tender.
5. Add beans, green chilies and tomatoes; return to a simmer, stirring often.
6. Cook about 5 minutes longer...liquid will reduce and thicken slightly.
7. Remove from heat and stir in cilantro.
8. Serve over brown rice

Yams grow in tropical and sub-tropical countries and require 8 – 10 months of warm weather to mature. The yam can grow up to seven feet and can range in color from off-white to brown.

ROASTED SWEET POTATO SOUP

4 medium sweet potatoes
2 tablespoons safflower oil
1 medium Vidalia onion, sliced
2 tablespoons ground black pepper
1 medium red bell pepper, seeded and thinly sliced
3 garlic cloves, finely chopped
4 cups water
2 vegetable bouillon cubes
1 tablespoon honey
¼ teaspoon curry powder

1. Preheat oven to 400o. Roast sweet potatoes on baking sheet until thoroughly done. Allow potatoes to cool then scoop cooked potato out of skins and set aside.
2. In a large soup pot, heat oil over medium heat. Add onion and cook until caramelized, stirring occasionally.
3. Add bell pepper and garlic. Cook for 5 minutes. Add sweet potato, black pepper and water; stir to combine. Add bouillon cubes and bring to boil. Reduce to a simmer and cook for 20 minutes.
4. Puree soup in a food processor or blender and pour into a clean pot. Add honey and curry powder, stirring for 1 minute. (Remove from heat and serve.

Sweet Potato Corn Soup

SWEET POTATO CORN SOUP

1 Tablespoon safflower oil
2 medium carrots, peeled and chopped
1 medium red onion, chopped
1 rib celery, chopped
1 red bell pepper, chopped
1 large sweet potato, peeled and chopped
1 sprig fresh thyme, minced
3/4 teaspoon ground turmeric
1 medium tomato, chopped

5 cups water
2 vegetable bouillon cubes
1 cup fresh or frozen corn kernels
3 cups stemmed and chopped kale leaves
1 tablespoon sea salt
Cayenne pepper, to taste
1 Tablespoon cornstarch
1 Tablespoon water

1. Heat oil in a large sauté pan over medium-high heat. Sauté carrots, red onions, celery, bell peppers, and sweet potato for 3 minutes. Add thyme and turmeric. Combine well with vegetables.
2. Add tomatoes, water and bouillon cubes; simmer 20 minutes.
3. Add corn, kale and sea salt. Simmer 5 minutes. Season to taste with cayenne pepper.
4. Combine cornstarch with 1 tablespoon water. With soup simmering, stir in cornstarch mixture. Continue to stir and simmer 3 minutes to thicken. Remove from heat and serve. Adapted from: _The Whole Foods Market Cookbook_ by Steve Petusevsky (Clarkson Potter)
http://homecooking.about.com/od/soups/r/blss150.htm

SPICED SWEET POTATO SOUP

2 tablespoon vegan butter
2 tablespoons fresh ginger, finely grated
1 cup chopped celery
2 cup chopped onion
1 tablespoon curry powder
¼ teaspoon cayenne pepper
1/8 teaspoon nutmeg
2 ½ pounds sweet potatoes, peeled and cut into ½ inch cubes
6 cups organic vegetable broth
½ teaspoon thyme
1 small bay leaf
½ teaspoon black pepper
½ cup almond milk

1. In a large pot over medium heat, melt margarine
2. Add ginger, celery and onion; cook approximately 5 minutes or until soft
3. Add curry powder, cinnamon, cayenne and nutmeg. Cook 1 minute, stirring constantly
4. Add sweet potatoes, broth, thyme, bay leaf and pepper.
5. Increase heat to high and bring to boil
6. Lower heat to medium and simmer 25 minutes or until potatoes are soft and cooked through
7. Puree soup in a blender or food processor
8. Add additional milk for thinning if needed.

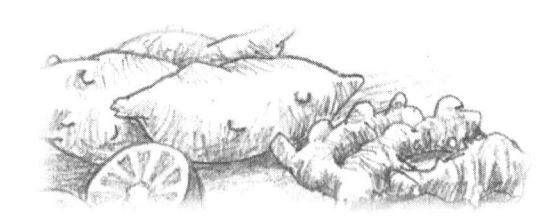

In addition to being a great source of complex carbohydrates, sweet potatoes are an important source of vitamin B6. Sweet potatoes contain the calcium and potassium, the minerals that your body needs to regulate heartbeat, blood pressure, and transmission of nerve impulses. They also contain significant amounts of folate.

Sweet Potato Salad

SWEET POTATO SALAD

2 pounds sweet potatoes, cooked, peeled and cut into bite sized cubes
½ cup dried cranberries
¼ cup raisins
¼ cup chopped walnuts
½ cup grapeseed vegenaise
1 tablespoon lemon juice
1 tablespoon orange juice
1 teaspoon grated orange peel
½ teaspoon grated ginger
¼ teaspoon nutmeg

1. In large bowl, combine, potatoes, cranberries, raisins and walnuts.
2. In small bowl, combine vegenaise, lemon juice, orange juice, orange peel, ginger and nutmeg
3. Fold juice mixture into potato mixture
4. Cover and chill for 2 hours

Sweet Potato Coleslaw

SWEET POTATO COLESLAW

3 cups shredded cabbage
2 medium sweet potatoes, shredded
1 cup carrots, shredded
¼ cup Poppy seed dressing
¼ cup grapeseed veganaise

1. In large bowl, combine cabbage, potatoes and carrots.
2. In small bowl, combine vegenaise and poppy seed dressing
3. Fold dressing mixture into cabbage mixture
4. Cover and chill for 1 hour

SWEET 'N SOUR SLAW

2 cups raw sweet potatoes cut into julienne strips
3 cups celery cut into julienne strips
¼ cup green onions sliced thin
2 tablespoon toasted sesame seeds
1 tablespoon orange juice
1/8 teaspoon cracked pepper
¼ cup safflower oil
2 tablespoons lemon juice
1 tablespoon agave nectar

1. In large bowl, combine sweet potatoes with the remaining ingredients
2. Toss to blend
3. Chill until ready to serve

Adapted from North Carolina Sweet Potato Commission

A ½ cup of cooked sweet potatoes provides approximately 25 micrograms of folate, which is about 14% of the recommended daily allowance. According to Albert Purcell (1971), an 8-ounce sweet potato provides nearly 1/5 of the minimum daily protein needs and a 2 ½ day supply of iron for women.

RED RUSSET SWEET POTATO SOUP

3 large sweet potatoes
2 medium russet potatoes
2 medium red potatoes
1 medium red onion, sliced
2 medium garlic gloves
3 celery stalks, sliced
1 teaspoon cumin
1 teaspoon oregano
2 teaspoons Herbamare
4 cup vegetable broth
1 cup almond milk

1. Boil and peel potatoes
2. In food processor, blend 3 cups water and potatoes, gradually adding onion, garlic, celery.
3. Transfer to stock pot add remaining ingredients and simmer

3
How Sweet It Is

"A seismic revolution in health will not come from a pill, procedure, or operation. It will occur when the public is endowed with nutritional literacy."

~ T. Colin Campbell, PhD & Caldwell B. Esselstyn, Jr. MD Foreword, Forks Over Knives

How Sweet it is – Natural Alternatives to Sugar

Sugar is the most popular food additive in the U.S. In 1915, the national average of sugar consumption (per year) was around 15 to 20 pounds per person. [3]By 1970, the average consumption was up to 123 pounds of sugar per year. According to reported U.S. Department of Agriculture (USDA) data, sugar consumption in 1999 was 30 percent higher than in 1983. Consumption has risen every year but one since 1983, while the World Health Organization (WHO) and the USDA continue to recommend we consume no more than 10% of our calories in added sugar.

There are many reasons to limit the amount of sugar that we eat including tooth decay, high triglycerides, diabetes, hypoglycemia and obesity. Add to that the fact that sweets often displace nutrient-dense fiber rich foods. For example; One pound of bananas (3 medium bananas) has the same amount of calories as a 2 ounce chocolate bar. Choosing the bananas gives you all the calories and fat of the chocolate bar with the additional benefit of vitamins, minerals and fiber not available in the chocolate bar.

There are many different names by which we know sugar representing its many forms: Brown Sugar, Corn Sweetener, Corn Syrup, Dextrose, Fructose, Fruit Juice Concentrate, Glucose, High-Fructose Corn Syrup, Lactose, Maltose, Molasses, Sorghum Syrup, Sucrose, and Syrup.

In the past a material called 'bone char' was used extensively to remove color from raw cane sugar in the refining process. Bone char is charcoal filter created by heating cow bones to 1200 o and grinding into charcoal. Modern technology has largely replaced bone char decolorisation but it is still used in a few refineries create white, brown and powdered sugars. However, it is not used in making white beet sugar and it is not used in making raw cane sugar. [4]

For newcomers transitioning from a SAD (Standard American Diet) nutritional approach to a plant based way of eating my best advice is to get the white out. Sweeteners, particularly refined sugars; are one of the greatest sources of empty calories with far reaching residual health effects. Refined sugars have been known to contribute to diabetes, poor eyesight, eczema and yeast infections. You are invited to view the 5 minute YouTube video entitled "How Sweet It Is" by visiting http://www.youtube.com/watch?v=-28NrqAUYw4

The following list will give you a team of health-friendly sweeteners to choose from and help you avoid conventional sugar.

EVAPORATED CANE JUICE is made by dehydrating the crystals left after cane juice has been pressed and is equally as sweet as white sugar. The evaporated cane juice crystals are a light tan color.

SUCANAT stands for **SU**gar **CA**ne **NAT**ural. This molasses flavor sweetener is not as sweet as sugar. It is made by crushing sugar cane, extracting the juice and rapidly evaporating the syrup to create a porous granule. Sucanat is great for baking, especially in chocolate-based recipes, b-b-q sauces and marinades. Also wonderful on hot cereals and in beverages. Use as a 1-1-replacement for refined sugar.

TURBINADO SUGAR a.k.a. raw sugar because of its tan colored coarse granules is made by steam cleaning unrefined sugar. Although most of the molasses content is removed during the cleaning process, the granules still impart a light molasses flavor.

AGAVE NECTAR made from the juice (aguamiel) of the agave plant. cactus-like Mexican agave plant. It has a very sweet taste, similar to maple syrup. It is sweeter than white sugar. This sweet liquid is less dense and not as sticky as honey. The lighter variety of agave is milder in flavor than the darker version, which tastes more like molasses. Agave is good for making sauces and custards. As a sweetener, agave nectar is touted as a glycemic superstar ringing in a glycemic load and index that is lower than most natural sweeteners on the market. However, Agave has been shown to be primarily fructose. According to Ronald Deis's 2001 article agave nectar is 92% fructose and 8% glucose. [5] The benefit is that agave is more slowly absorbed into the bloodstream than table sugar. Additionally, you end up using less because agave is sweeter than sugar.

BROWN RICE SYRUP is made from sprouted brown rice. This traditional Asian sweetener is thick and golden brown syrup. It has a nutty, butterscotch-like flavor that is mild and not as sweet as white sugar.

It is recommended for people who have blood sugar problems.

HONEY, a powerful immune system builder with anti-allergy properties, comes in many varieties and flavors. The anti-allergy properties are specific to your area; which is why it is better to buy honey from a local source. Local honey may help with seasonal allergies because it contains bits of pollen from the plants, thereby reducing your allergy symptoms to local flowering plants. (add endnote 6 and renumber)

MAPLE SYRUP is the natural sweetener with the least amount of calories. The color and flavor are used to assess grade to this natural sweetener, with Grade A being the most superior.

STEVIA is extracted from a South African shrub. Although it is very sweet it has been reported to have a metallic aftertaste. Research raises questions around safety as high doses used in animals have resulted in fertility and metabolic problems. However, some studies have shown that stevia can lower blood sugar and help control your blood pressure. [6]

BLACKSTRAP MOLASSES is a thick syrupy by-product of the sugar-making process. Half as sweet as white sugar, this intensely flavored sweetener is a little bitterer than light or dark molasses. Unrefined, organic brands that do not use bone char are the best choice.

BARLEY MALT SYRUP, robust sweetener that works well in muffins, cakes, and sweet breads. When cooking it is important to remember that not all substitutes are one-for-one ratio with conventional sugar. The following culinary use conversion table will help.

	EVAPORATED CANE JUICE	SUCANAT	TURBINADO SUGAR	AGAVE	BLACKSTRAP MOLASSES	BROWN RICE SYRUP	MAPLE SYRUP
Ratio with conventional sugar	1 cup:1 cup sugar	1 cup:1 cup sugar	1 cup:1 cup sugar	2/3 cup:1 cup sugar (reduce other recipe liquid by 1/3 cup)	2 cups:1 cup sugar (reduce other recipe liquid by 1/3 cup)	1 ¼ cups:1 cup sugar (reduce other recipe liquid by 1/3 cup)	2/3 cup: 1 cup sugar (reduce other recipe liquid by 1/3 cup)
Best uses	Works well in pie fillings, meringues, pie fillings and custards as well as jellies and sauces.	In addition to Marinades it works well with chocolate-based recipes.	Can be used in a variety of foods, particularly hot beverages, cereals and baked goods.	Can be used in a variety of foods as well as hot or cold liquids. Excellent in baked goods and sauces.	Best used in sauces and marinades, cookies and baked beans.	Works well in baking and beverages both hot and cold.	A wonderful replacement for honey, maple syrup is great in baked goods and sauces. The darkest variety of maple syrup is Grade B, which is the best for cooking
Nutrition Nugget	Evaporated cane juice contains iron.	Contains iron, calcium, potassium, vitamin B_6 and chromium.	Contains trace amounts of iron and calcium.	Blood sugar levels do not rise as high or as quickly as with white sugar	Blackstrap molasses contains iron, calcium, vitamin B_6 and magnesium.	Contain complex carbohydrates which results in slow and steady rise of blood sugar levels.	Contains calcium, potassium, magnesium, manganese, phosphorus and iron

Vegetarian Times October 2004

ALMOND MILK

3 cups raw almonds, soaked overnight, drained and skinned
6 dates, pitted
7 cups of water
2 teaspoon ground cinnamon
2 teaspoon organic vanilla extract

1. Combine all ingredients in a blender.
2. Blend until smooth
3. Strain ingredients through a piece of cheesecloth into a glass container. Yields 4 servings and will keep in the refrigerator for approximately 5 days.

Sweet potatoes contain minerals that your body needs to regulate heartbeat, blood pressure, and transmission of nerve impulses (calcium & potassium).

4 SWEETS & TREATS

He that takes medicine and neglects diet, waste the time of his doctor.

~ Ancient Chinese Proverb

Sweets and Treats

Your taste buds will be dazzled while your heart and energy will dance, all while savoring the following sweet tooth delights.

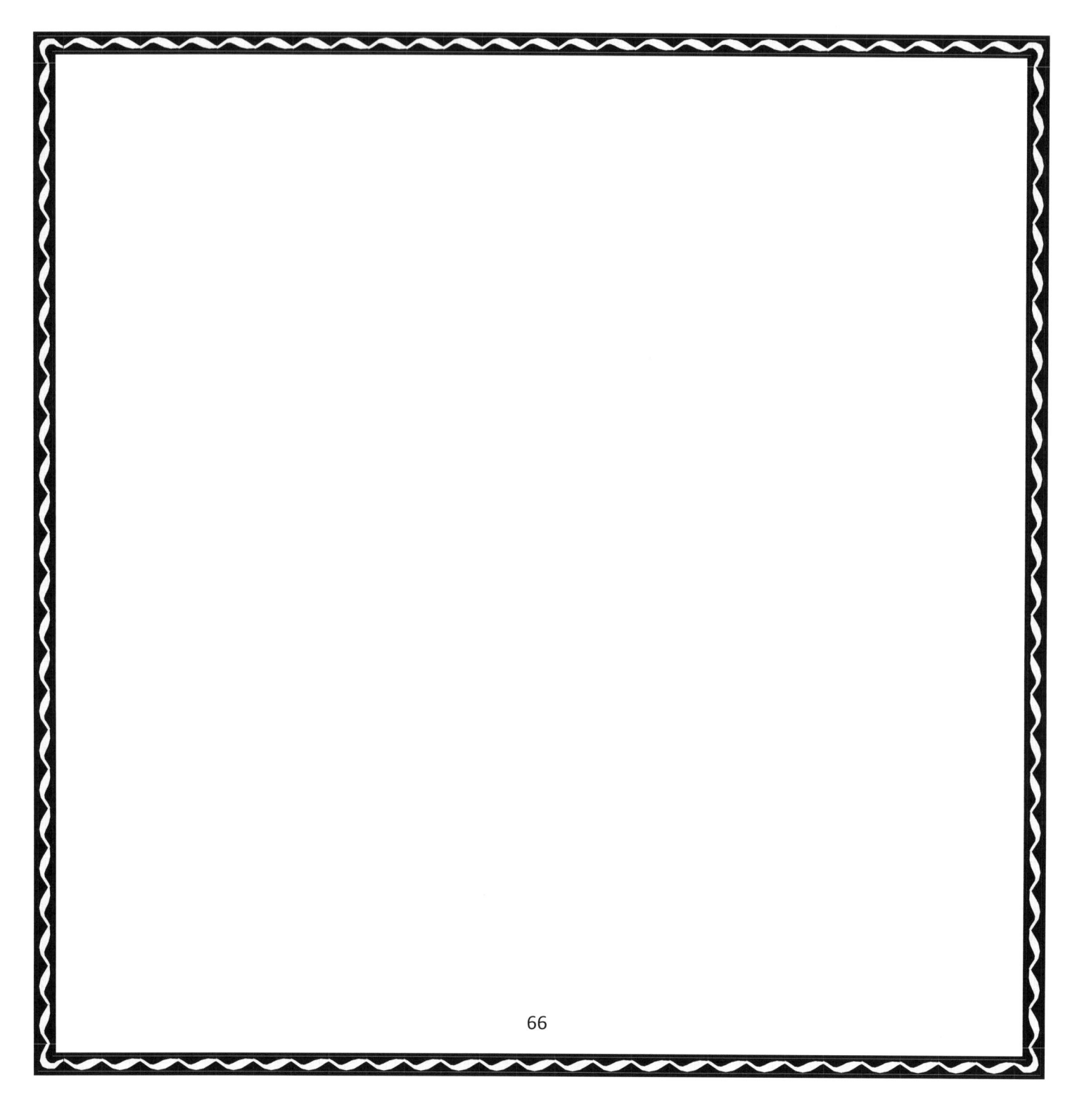

SWEET POTATO CHEESECAKE

2 – six-ounce organic graham cracker crust (wholly wholesome)
2 cup cooked mashed sweet potatoes
2 – eight ounce packages lite cream cheese, at room temperature
1 cup agave nectar
½ cup egg substitute
½ cup almond milk
½ teaspoon cinnamon
2 teaspoon vanilla extract
¼ teaspoon nutmeg
2 tablespoons cornstarch

1. Preheat oven to 350°F
2. In a large bowl, beat cream cheese and agave until fluffy
3. Beat in egg substitute and almond milk.
4. Add mashed sweet potatoes. Mix well
5. Add cornstarch, cinnamon, nutmeg and vanilla. Blend well
6. Pour batter into pie crusts.
7. Bake for approximately 1 hour or until center is almost set
8. Remove from heat and cool at least 1 hour.

Sweet Potato Muffins

SWEET POTATO MUFFINS

1 Cup Earth balance (vegan butter)
2 cups Agave nectar
2-½ cup cooked, mashed sweet potatoes
3 tablespoon prepared EnerG vegan egg substitute
2 teaspoon vanilla extract
3 cups whole wheat flour
1 teaspoon baking soda
1 teaspoon lemon extract
1 teaspoon nutmeg
1 teaspoon cinnamon

1. Preheat oven to 350°F.
2. In a large bowl, cream together butter with agave nectar.
3. Add sweet potatoes, EnerG, and vanilla and beat for 2 minute
4. Add remaining ingredients and mix well
5. Pour batter into prepared muffin pan
6. Bake 30 – 45 minutes or until toothpick inserted into the center comes out clean.

SWEET POTATO CUPCAKES

1 Cup Earth balance (vegan butter)
2 cups Agave nectar
2-½ cup cooked, mashed sweet potatoes
3 tablespoon prepared EnerG vegan egg substitute
2 teaspoon vanilla extract
3 cups oat flour
1 teaspoon baking soda
1 teaspoon nutmeg
1 teaspoon cinnamon
1 cup golden raisins or dried cranberries

1. Preheat oven to 350°F.
2. In a large bowl, cream together butter with agave nectar.
3. Add sweet potatoes, EnerG, and vanilla and beat for 2 minute
4. Add flour, baking soda, nutmeg and cinnamon. Mix well
5. Fold in raisins/cranberries
6. Spoon into cupcake molds

**Bake approx 45 minutes or until toothpick inserted into the center comes out clean.

SWEET POTATO BROWNIES

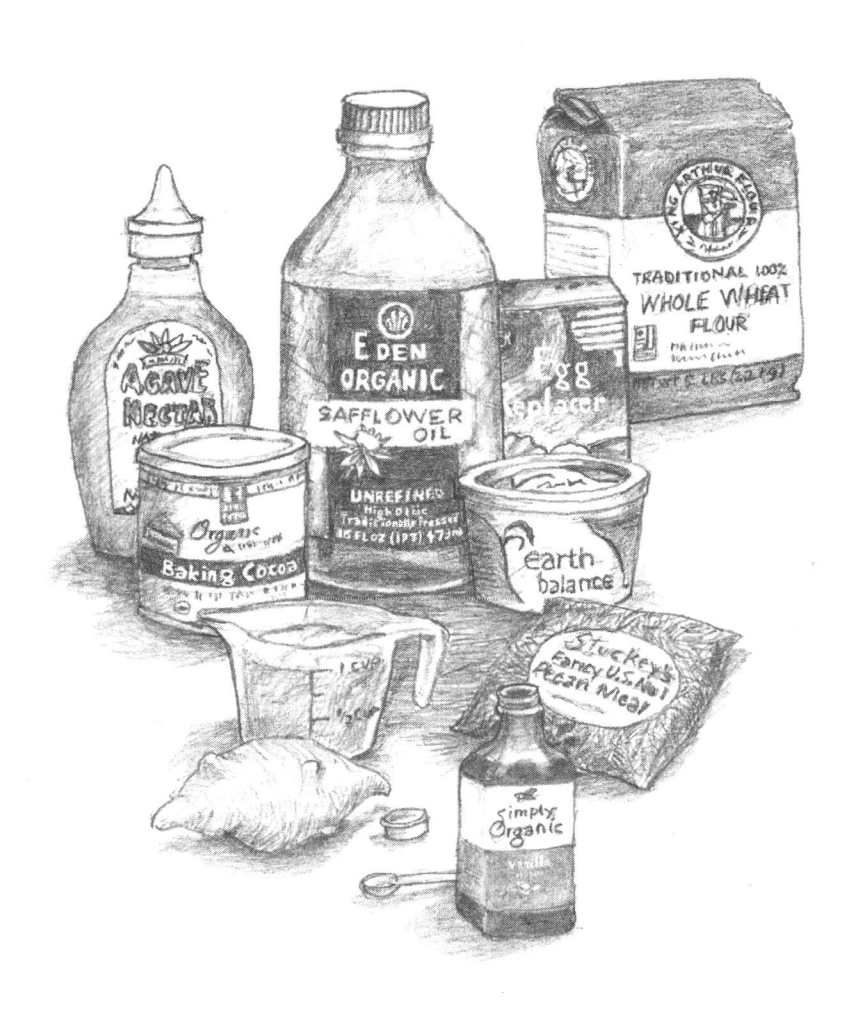

SWEET POTATO BROWNIES

1/2 cup non-hydrogenated butter (Earth balance)
1 cup Agave nectar
3 tablespoons prepared EggReplacer®*
1 teaspoon organic vanilla extract
¾ cup organic whole wheat flour
½ cup prepared organic bakers cocoa
1 cup mashed sweet potatoes
½ cup pecan meal (or chopped unsalted dry roasted pecans)
1 teaspoon safflower oil
*(3tbsp Ener-GEgg Replacer +1/3 cup water)

1. Preheat oven to 350°F. Grease a 9x13-inch baking pan.
2. In a large bowl, cream together butter with agave nectar.
3. Add EggReplacer and beat for 1 minute
4. Fold in the rest of the ingredients
5. Spread batter in pan
6. Bake 30 – 45 minutes or until toothpick inserted into the center comes out clean. Serves 16.

**To serve only 8, half the recipe ingredients and use an 8x8 pan.*

SWEET POTATO POUND CAKE

1 cup soy margarine (earth balance buttery sticks)
1 cup evaporated cane juice
2/3 cup agave nectar
2 ½ cup cooked mashed sweet potatoes
2/3 cup egg replacer (ener-g)
2 teaspoon vanilla
3 cups unbleached whole wheat flor
1 teaspoon baking soda
1 teaspoon lemon extract
1 teaspoon nutmeg
1 teaspoon cinnamon

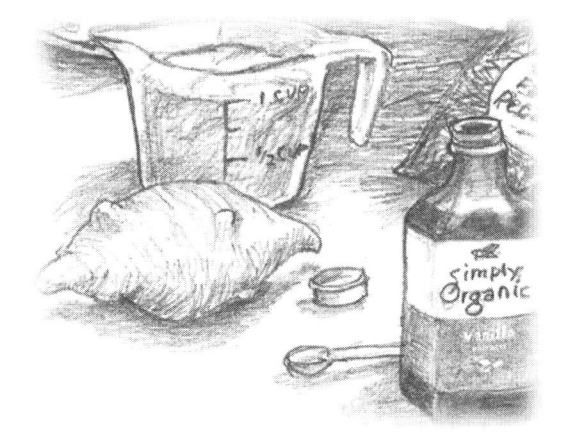

1. Heat oven to 350°F
2. Cream margarine and cane juice until fluffy
3. Add agave nectar and beat for 1 minute
4. Add sweet potatoes, egg replacer and vanilla. Beat for 2 minutes
5. Add remaining ingredients and mix well
6. Pour batter into nonstick loaf pan
7. Bake for 1 hour or until inserted toothpick comes out clean

CRANBERRY SWEET POTATO CAKE

3 Cups Organic Whole Wheat Pastry Flour
1 ¼ Cups Natural Cane Turbinado sugar
1 Tablespoon baking soda
2 teaspoons cinnamon
1 ½ teaspoons ground ginger
¾ teaspoon ground nutmeg
½ Teaspoon sea salt
2 cup sweet potato puree
1 Cup water
¼ Cup safflower oil
2 Tablespoons Bragg organic apple cider vinegar
2 teaspoons vanilla extract
1 Cup dried cranberries

RUM BUTTERCREAM ICING
2/3 Cup vegan margarine
4 Cups powdered sugar
¼ Cup almond milk
2 teaspoons light rum (or rum extract)
½ Cup pecan meal

CARROT CAKE WITH CREAM CHEESE ICING

3 teaspoons lemon juice
1 1/4 cups almond milk
2/3 cup safflower oil
2 teaspoons orange zest
1 cup agave nectar
3 teaspoons vanilla extract
3 cups oat flour
1 1/2 teaspoons baking powder
1 1/2 teaspoons ground cinnamon
2 cups grated carrots

1/2 cup chopped walnuts

Cream Cheese Frosting:
1 - 8 oz cream cheese (Tofutti Better Than Cream Cheese)
1/2 cup almond milk
2 cups sweetener
1 tsp vanilla extract
2 tsp lemon juice
½ cup cranberries

Combine the cream cheese and margarine. Slowly add the powdered sugar, then vanilla and lemon juice

1. Preheat oven to 350 degrees F (175 degrees C). Prepare Bundt pan.
2. In a small bowl stir together lemon juice and milk.
3. Let stand 5 minutes.
4. Sift flour, baking powder, cinnamon together and set aside.
5. In a large bowl, cream oil, orange zest and agave. Add milk mixture and vanilla.
6. Add flour mixture and beat until smooth. Stir in the grated carrots and chopped nuts.
7. Pour the batter into pan.
8. Bake at 350 degrees F (175 degrees C) for 1 hour, or until a toothpick inserted into the cake comes out clean. Allow to cool.

SWEET POTATO COOKIES

1 cup Cranberries
¼ cup Earth Balance
1 cup Cooked sweet potatoes, mashed
1 cup Egg beaters
1 teaspoon vanilla
2 cups Whole wheat flour
½ teaspoon sea salt
¼ cup sucanat
½ teaspoon nutmeg
½ teaspoon baking soda
1 teaspoon cinnamon
½ cup rolled oats
¼ cup pecans or walnuts (optional)
Organic canola oil spray

1. Preheat oven to 350~.
2. Cream Earth Balance, then add sweet potato, egg, & vanilla; beat till creamy.
3. Mix flour, sea salt, sucanat, nutmeg, baking soda, baking powder and cinnamon.
4. Add to creamed mixture and mix well.
5. Add cranberries, rolled oats and nuts.
6. Drop onto cookie sheet sprayed w/canola cooking spray.
7. Bake 12 min or until done.

AVOCADO KEY LIME PIE

4 ½ ripe avocados
1/2 cup agave nectar
2/3 cup freshly squeezed lime juice
6 tablespoons melted coconut oil
¼ teaspoon vanilla

1. Combine avocado, agave nectar, lime juice and vanilla in the food processor.
2. Blend until creamy and smooth, slowly adding melted coconut.
3. Pour into pecan pie crust.
4. Let sit in the refrigerator for at least 30 minutes to firm up a bit.

PECAN-HAZELNUT PIE CRUST

1 cup grounded hazelnuts
1 cup pecans finely chopped
4 tablespoons agave nectar
2 tablespoons melted coconut oil
3 teaspoons cinnamon
¼ taspoon nutmeg
½ teaspoon vanilla extract

1. Preheat oven to 350 degrees Fahrenheit
2. Combine nuts, cinnamon and nutmeg in a bowl.
3. Whisk together melted coconut oil, agave and vanilla then add to nut mixture
4. Press mixture into pie plate
5. Bake about 10 minute
6. Allow crust to cool completely before adding pie filling

Adapted from http:www.zupas.com/index.php/2010/02/recipe-hazelnut-and-pecan-pie-crust/

~The doctor of the future will give no medication, but will interest his patients in the care of the human frame, in diet, and the cause and prevention of disease." ~ Thomas Edison *THE FUTURE IS NOW and YOU are the doctor!*

SWEET POTATO COBBLER

2 cups sweet potato, cooked and cubed
2/3 cup sorghum molasses
½ cup almond milk
½ cup vegan butter
½ teaspoon ginger
¼ teaspoon cinnamon
1 teaspoon vanilla
1 roll prepared biscuit dough

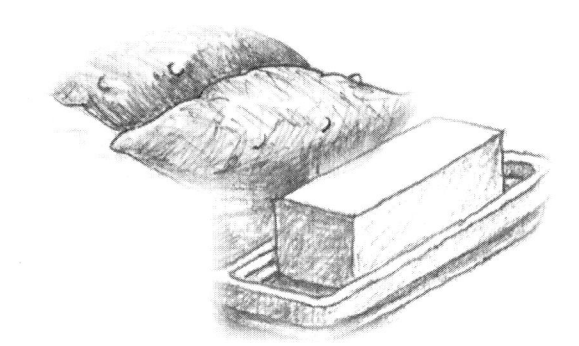

1. Preheat oven to 400°
2. Mix potatoes, molasses, butter, milk and spices together in a large saucepan and bring to a boil.
3. Cut part of rolled dough into cubes and stir into potato mixture.
4. Pour mixture into casserole dish.
5. Cut remaining dough into thin slices and place on top of potato mixture.
6. Bake until the crust is golden brown.

JAMAICAN SWEET POTATO PUDDING CAKE

For the cake:
1 cup raisins
2 tablespoons dark or light rum
1 cup whole-wheat pastry flour
1/2 teaspoon freshly grated nutmeg
1/2 teaspoon sea salt
2 medium sweet potatoes, cooked, peeled and mashed.
3 large eggs

1 ½ cup coconut milk
1 cup sorghum molasses
2 tablespoons vegan butter, softened

For the topping:
1/2 cup unsweetened shredded coconut
2 tablespoons evaporated cane juice
1/8 teaspoon ground cinnamon

Preheat oven to 350°F.

To prepare cake:
1. Toss raisins and rum in a small bowl and set aside. Whisk flour, nutmeg and salt in another bowl. In a large bowl combine mashed sweet potato and egg substitute. Beat with an electric mixer on medium speed until combined.
2. Add coconut milk, molasses and butter; beat until combined. Stir in dry ingredients until evenly moistened. Stir in raisins and any remaining rum. Spread batter in prepared 9 inch pan.

To prepare topping:
1. Combine coconut, 2 tablespoons cane sugar and cinnamon in a small bowl. Sprinkle on top of cake. Bake cake 1 hour, until a knife inserted into center comes out clean. Let cool in pan for 10 minutes.
2. Run a knife around the edge of the pan and gently remove. Let cool at room temperature for 1 hour, refrigerate for about 3 hours then slice and serve.
Adapted from:
http://www.lifescript.com/Body/Food/Cook/7_Sweet_Potato_Recipes.aspx

ALMOND CREAM

Almonds
Water
1 tablespoon Agave or maple syrup

1. Soak almonds 24 hours, discard water
2. Heat 2 cups water to boiling
3. Dip almonds in heated water
4. Immediately drain and run cold water on them
5. Pop almonds out of skin
6. Fill blender with 2 cups of almonds
7. Add 1 cup water & blend
8. Add 3 tablespoon agave
9. Use in place of whip cream

Courtesy of Thelma Raziya Curtis
Healing Support Network, Inc./Raziya's Rolling Pantry

The 1971 article "Sweet Potato: The Versatile Vegetable", by Albert Purcell, reported the use of sweet potatoes as a replacement for wheat in making bread and its fermentation for alcoholic beverages and various commercial solvents. The plethora of products and usages for this phenomenal gift of nature is amazing. From the medical lab to the medical doctor, from the office to the kitchen, the sweet potato has become useful in many areas of life. Nature's health food is always a welcome addition to your plate, however you prepare it.

SWEET POTATO PUDDING

2 large sweet potatoes
2 cups pitted dates
½ teaspoon nutmeg
½ teaspoon cinnamon
1 teaspoon allspice
1 cup orange juice
2 teaspoon organic vanilla extract

OPTIONAL:
1 cup pine nuts (soak for 6 hours)

1. Soak dates in 1 cup water for 2 hours
2. Peel and cut sweet potatoes so they fit in food processor
3. Feed sweet potatoes, dates (and pine nuts) in processor, adding alternately
4. Add remaining ingredients
5. Combine thoroughly
6. Serve topped with almond cream

ALMOND CREAM see page _____

Courtesy of Thelma Raziya Curtis
Healing Support Network, Inc./Raziya's Rolling Pantry

Cooking with Tempeh

What is tempeh!? Tempeh, like tofu, is made from soybeans – but it actually has a higher nutritional content than tofu. It uses the whole soybean, and a fermentation process causes the tempeh to maintain a higher and more easily digestible protein content than tofu. The soybeans are packed into a cake that's easy to slice and cook with, and the high protein content makes it a fantastic alternative to meat (and it has no cholesterol). You will love the nutty, savory flavor.

There are several reasons to choose fermented soy like tempeh over unfermented soy like tofu. First and foremost science has shown that the body's absorption of minerals is blocked by substances contained in unfermented soy. Secondly, unfermented soy contains enzyme inhibitors that disrupt protein digestion and also contain high amounts of omega-6 fats which promote inflammation. Other concerns with unfermented soy include possible blocking of the hormone estrogen and depressed thyroid gland (which can lead to weight gain, lethargy, fatigue, hair loss and loss of libido). Choosing fermented soy, like tempeh is better because the long process of fermentation results in all those negative substances mentioned above being greatly reduced and their beneficial properties become available to your digestive system.

Tempeh also contains a high amount of essential fatty acids, fiber, vitamins and minerals. The fact that tempeh keeps the whole soybean intact and is less processed than tofu makes it a more nutritious choice.

Tempeh can be used in place of bacon in a vegetarian BLT, as a substitute for sausage or meat crumbles in tacos or breakfast dishes, and as a mouth-watering addition to stir-fry and quinoa or brown rice dishes. Throw it into a pan with a bit of oil until it is crispy and browned. Add your favorite spices and seasonings and you've got a great meal!

There are even different flavors of tempeh – some that add ground flax seeds (high in omega 3's) and garden vegetables. Make sure you buy organic tempeh so you know it hasn't been made with GMO soybeans.

The last thing to consider when grocery shopping for tempeh, is whether to buy fermented or non-fermented. More info to follow.

SOURCE: http://healthycrush.com/tempeh-101/

One quarter of what you eat keeps you alive. The other three quarters keep your doctor alive.
~EYGPTIAN PROVERB

5

TEMPEH RECIPES

TEMPEH PASTA SALAD

1 – 8 oz Tempeh bar
2 tablespoons grated ginger
½ cup Braggs amino
1 cup water
2 tablespoon Sesame Seed oil
2 tablespoon Safflower oil
½ cup Broccoli flowerettes
½ cup Cauliflower flowerettes
½ cup red bell pepper, chopped fine
Annie's Goddess Dressing

1. Place tempeh in a shallow dish
2. Stir together ginger, Braggs and water.
3. Pour ginger mixture over tempeh and marinade for 2 – 24 hours
4. Remove from marinade and cut into bite size cubes
5. Prepare pasta, al dente
6. Steam broccoli & cauliflower
7. In large bowl toss pasta and broccoli mixture and set aside
8. Heat oil in pan and sauté tempeh for approximately 15 minutes, stirring often
9. Top pasta mixture with browned tempeh
10. Sprinkle bell peppers on top of pasta and tempeh
11. Add dressing to taste

Adapted from Raziya Curtis September 2011

TLT (TEMPEH, LETTUCE & TOMATO) SANDWICH

1 - 8 ounce block of tempeh, cut into 1/3-inch thick strips, marinated
2 tbsp. safflower oil
1 small bunch of red-leaf lettuce, shredded
4 medium vine ripe tomatoes, sliced
2 large avocados, mashed with a pinch of sea salt just before assembling
8 pieces of hearty whole grain bread, thinly sliced and lightly toasted (4 sandwiches)

When the tempeh is done marinating heat oil in a large pan over medium-high heat
Cook the tempeh slices for 3 – 5 minutes on each side.

1. Set the tempeh slices aside until you are ready to assemble the sandwiches.
2. To assemble each sandwich
3. Spread a layer of mashed avocado on one slice of bread
4. Place a small helping of the shredded lettuce on top of the avocado
5. Place 2-3 slices of tomatoes on top of avocado, then a few slices of the tempeh
6. Place 2-3 slices of tomatoes on top of tempeh
7. Top with another avocado-slathered slice of bread
8. Cut in half & serve.

TEMPEH MARINADE

3 tablespoons safflower oil
1/4 cup Braggs liquid amino
2 tablespoons balsamic vinegar
2 tablespoons sorghum molasses (or maple syrup)
3 tablespoons chipotle adobo sauce (optional, recipe below)

1. Whisk together the safflower oil, Bragg aminos, balsamic vinegar, molasses and adobo sauce.
2. Place tempeh into a baking dish large enough to hold the tempeh in a single layer.
3. Pour the marinade over the tempeh
4. Cover and keep in the refrigerator for 2 – 24 hours, until ready to use

CHIPOLTE ADOBO SAUCE
7 medium dried chipotle peppers, stems removed
1/3 cup sliced onion
5 tbsp. apple cider vinegar
2 cloves of garlic
¼ cup of organic catsup
3 cups water

1. Simmer all the ingredients over very low heat for an hour to an hour and a half.

TEMPEH JAMBALAYA

1 - 8 ounce block of multigrain tempeh
¼ cup safflower oil, divided
2 tbsps. Creole seasoning (recipe below)
2 tbsps. Bragg amino (or organic tamari sauce)
1 small sweet onion chopped
2 celery stalks, diced
1 small green bell pepper, deseeded and diced
1 small red bell pepper, deseeded and diced
1 jalapeno pepper, deseeded and diced

1 ½ cups jasmine rice (or brown basmati rice)
2 garlic cloves, minced
2 vegan vegetable bouillon (sea salt & herbs) dissolved in 2 cups water
3 medium tomatoes deseeded and diced (or 1 - 14 oz. can organic diced tomatoes)
1 bay leaf
1 - 15 ounce can organic red beans, drained and rinsed
½ cup green onion, thinly sliced

1. In a large pot, heat 2 Tsp. safflower oil over medium heat.
2. Crumble the tempeh into small pieces into pot and sauté the tempeh for 5 minutes.
3. Sprinkle 1 Tsp. creole seasoning over the tempeh and sauté an additional 1 minute.
4. Add Bragg amino, stir well to coat the tempeh and continue to cook until the liquid has evaporated.
5. Transfer the tempeh to a plate and set aside.
6. In the same pot, sauté the onion, celery, green pepper, red pepper, and jalapeno in the remaining 2 Tbsp. safflower oil until soften.
7. Add the rice and garlic, stir well to combine, and continue to cook an additional 2-3
8. Add the vegetable stock, tomatoes, remaining Creole Seasoning, bay leaf and bring the mixture to a boil.
9. Cover, reduce the heat to low, simmer for 20-25 minutes or until the rice is tender and most of the liquid is absorbed.
10. Remove the lid, add the reserved tempeh and remaining ingredients, stir well to combine, and recover the pot.

11. Remove the pot from the heat and let sit for 10 minutes to allow the flavors to blend.
12. Can be served as a side dish, main dish, or as a filling for wraps or sandwiches

CREOLE SEASONING
1 tbsp. Cayenne pepper
1 tbsp. Black pepper
1 tsp. Paprika
½ tsp. Dried Thyme
½ tsp. Dried Oregano
½ tsp. Garlic powder
½ tsp. Onion powder.

Mix all ingredients together

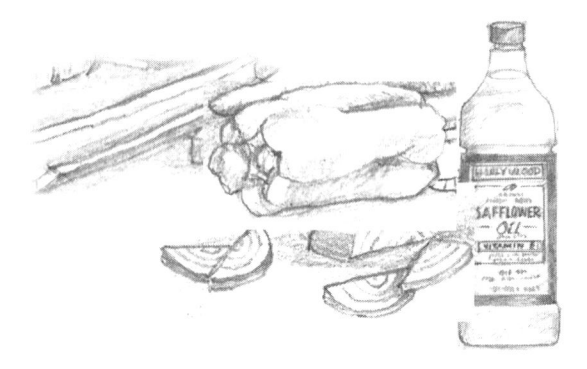

ITALIAN TEMPEH NUGGETS

1 - 8 ounce block of tempeh, cut into ½ inch wide cubes

For the Marinade
2 tbsps. Balsamic vinegar
2 tbsps. Bragg aminos
2 garlic cloves, minced
½ tsp. crushed red pepper
1 tsp. dried thyme
1 tsp. dried rosemary

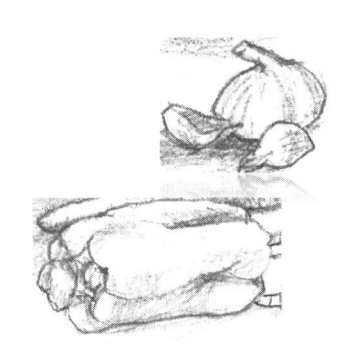

1. Combine all ingredients in a container with a lid, stir to combine.
2. Add tempeh, cover and shake well until all pieces are coated.
3. Place in refrigerator and marinade for 1 – 24 hours.
4. When ready to cook, heat medium skillet over medium-low heat.
5. Add tempeh and marinade liquid and cook for about 10 minutes, turning pieces until they begin to caramelize.
6. Serve immediately with a vegetable stir-fry, a tossed green salad or as an appetizer.

NAVY BEAN SOUP

16 ounces navy beans -- rinsed
8 cups water
2 garlic cloves
1 cup carrots, finely chopped
1 cup celery -- finely chopped & leaves
1/2 cup onion, finely chopped
2 vegetable bouillon cubes (Rupunzel vegan vegetable bouillon w/sea salt & herbs)
2-4 bay leaves
Black pepper
Allspice
Herbamare

1. In large saucepan or Dutch oven, combine all ingredients except seasoning
2. Bring to a boil. Boil 30 minutes.
3. Remove from heat. Let stand 1-1/2 hours or until beans are tender.
4. Spoon beans and vegetables into food processor.
5. Blend until smooth adding water as needed.
6. Add pepper, allspice and Herbamare to taste.

VEGETABLE CHILI

http://recipes.aarp.org/recipes/vegetarian-chili

1 tablespoon canola oil or olive oil
2 medium onions, chopped (about 12 ounces)
2 garlic cloves, minced
1 large green bell pepper; cored, seeded, and diced (about 8 ounces)
1 large red bell pepper; cored, seeded, and diced (about 8 ounces)
1 large zucchini, diced (about 8 ounces)
1 large yellow squash, diced (about 8 ounces)
2 large Portobello mushrooms, diced
15 ounces canned diced tomatoes
1½ cups vegetable stock (low-fat and low-sodium)
12 ounces corn kernels
3 cups cooked kidney beans or pinto beans
1 teaspoon dried thyme
1 teaspoon dried oregano
2 teaspoons ground cumin
2 tablespoons chili powder
¼ teaspoon cayenne pepper

Salt to taste
Cornstarch with a little water

1. Heat the oil in a deep pan over medium heat. Add the onions, garlic, and sauté for 2 minutes. Add the bell pepper, zucchini, yellow squash, mushrooms, diced tomatoes, stock, spices, herbs, and bring to a boil.
2. Reduce heat and simmer until the vegetables are tender. Pass through a sieve and return the liquid to the pan.
3. Reduce over high heat to concentrate the flavors and adjust seasoning. If needed, thicken with a little cornstarch water mixture.
4. Return the vegetables to the reduced liquid and serve immediately.

NAVY BEAN SQUASH SOUP

http://www.cdkitchen.com/recipes/recs/365/Navy-Bean-Squash-Soup81631.shtml

1 pound dry navy beans, sorted and rinsed
2 cans (14 1/2 oz each) chicken broth
2 cups water
1 meaty ham bone
2 pounds butternut squash, peeled, seeded and cubed
1 large onion, chopped
1/2 teaspoon salt
1/2 teaspoon black pepper

1. Place beans in a large saucepan or Dutch oven; add water to cover by 2 in. Bring to a boil; boil for 2 minutes.
2. Remove from heat; cover and let stand for 1 hour. Drain and discard liquid; return beans to pan.
3. Add the broth, water, ham bone, squash, onion, salt and pepper. Bring to a boil.
4. Reduce heat; cover and simmer for 1 1/2 to 1 3/4 hours or until beans are tender. Remove ham bone. Mash the soup mixture, leaving some chunks if desired.
5. Remove ham from bone; cut into chunks. Discard bone and fat. Return meat to the soup; heat through.

Awesome Rawsome

Processing and cooking is known to destroy enzymes in food. Although research has shown that some nutrients are enhanced by cooking while others are destroyed, for the purpose of this chapter, our emphasis will be on the benefits of raw food preparation.

Enzymes are a nutrient of concern for this discussion. What's the big fuss about enzymes? First and foremost, enzymes are needed for every chemical reaction that occurs in our body. "Think of it this way: enzymes are the labor force that builds your body just like construction workers are the labor force that builds your house. Similarly, you may have all the necessary building materials and lumber, but to build a house you need workers, which represent which represent the vital life element. Similarly, you may have all the nutrients (vitamins, proteins, etc) for your body, but you still need the enzymes, aka-the life element, to keep the body alive and well.

In other word, whatever you are eating, the enzymes are enhanced whenever they can be consumed in their most natural state. As long as the heat is no more than 118 degrees, the enzymes stay in tact and our bodies will benefit. The bottom line is that eating a diet of cooked and process foods places more stress on the body than the uncooked version of the same food. And isn't it the point to eat healthy for an increased immune system so that the body can work smarter not harder.

Here's to longevity.

EVERY CELL IN YOUR BODY IS EAVESDROPPING ON YOUR THOUGHTS. ~Deepak Choprah

6

AWESOME RAWSOME

GROUND CHERRY SALSA

2 cups of ground cherries, halved
1 small Red onion, diced (1/2 cup)
1/2 small jalapeno pepper, diced
1 tbsp cilantro, chopped
1 med red bell pepper, diced
1 small green bell pepper, diced
¼ tsp lime juice
1 tsp Extra Virgin olive oil
Pinch sea salt

1. Mix everything together and let sit for 30 minutes so the flavors can come together.

Adapted from: http://catertots.net/by-type/vegetable/ground-cherry-salsa
Dedicated to The Greening of Detroit's Garden Resource Program and my dear friend Althalene Moss

NO BAKE COOKIES

2 cups cane sugar
6 tablespoons chocolate chips
½ cups earth balance (or I Can't Believe It's Not Butter or Smart Balance)
½ cups almond milk
3 cups uncooked oatmeal
¾ cup organic creamy peanut butter
1 teaspoon vanilla

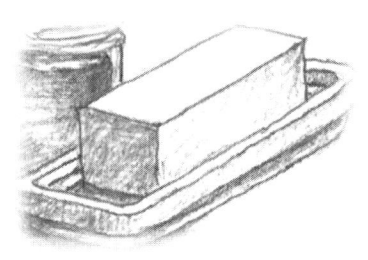

1. Combine sugar, chocolate chips, earth balance and almond milk in a large saucepan
2. Bring to boil on medium heat, stirring frequently for 3 minutes
3. Remove from heat and mix in oatmeal, peanut butter and vanilla
4. Line a cookie sheet with wax paper
5. Scoop mixture onto cookie sheet (1 heaping tablespoon per cookie)
6. Let set for 30 – 45 minutes

BUTTERNUT SQUASH SOUP

4 cups fresh orange juice
1 mango, peeled & chopped
4 cups butternut squash, small chunks
8 dates, pitted & chopped
1 teaspoon curry

1. Combine ingredients in blender.
2. Add water as needed for desired thickness
3. Serve

From the kitchen of Raziyah Curtis

RAWSOME SWEET POTATO CHEESECAKE

CRUST:

1 cup walnuts

1 cup macadamia nuts

½ cup pitted medjool dates

FILLING:

1 med sweet potato, peeled and cut into chunks

3 cups cashews, soaked in water for 1 hour

½ cup water

¾ cup virgin coconut oil

Fresh juice of 4 limes

¾ cup agave nectar or sorghum molasses

1 teaspoon vanilla extract

TO MAKE CRUST:
1. Combine walnuts, macadamia nuts and dates in a food processor.
2. Process using an S blade until well mixed.
3. Press the "dough" into the bottom of a 9 inch pie pan and set aside.

TO MAKE FILLING:
1. Place sweet potato chunks and ¼ cup coconut oil in food processor and process until smooth.
2. Add cashews, water, lime juice, sweetener, vanilla and remaining coconut oil and process until smooth and creamy.
3. Pour sweet potato mixture into the crust.
4. Place pie in freezer and freeze about 2 hours until firm.

7

PLANT-BASED EATING MADE EASY

Plant-Based Eating

Your success with plant based eating starts with the mind and moves to the kitchen. The fact that you have picked up this book tells me that you are already in the mindset to "eat to live". Having the essential gear in your kitchen will make all the difference in the ease with which you master and enjoy preparing plant-based dishes, delights and full course meals. You may need to "fake it 'til you make it" at the onset, but eventually you will want to have every tool listed below.

Keep your eyes open for good sales :~)

Tools of the Trade...

- 2 quart glass baking dish
- Baking sheets
- Blender
- Bowls – stainless steel
- Cheesecloth
- Colander
- Cutting boards – large thick wood (vegetables), medium-sized wood (fruit), plastic (seafood)
- Food Processor
- Grater
- Grinder
- Knives (good chef's knives)
- Ladles
- Measuring cups
- Measuring spoons
- Peeler
- Pepper mill
- Pots & pans (cast iron, stainless steel: a 10-inch fry pan, 2 saucepans w/lids, 1 large stockpot w/lid
- Salad spinner
- Sieves
- Spatulas (wooden & rubber)
- Spoons (wooden & stainless steel)
- Tongs
- Whisks

AFTERWORD

It has been said that when you know better you do better.

In 1999, when I first embarked on this sweet potato journey there was only a little buzz about the health benefits and medicinal properties of the wild yams, the starchier, drier cousin to the sweet potato. Some ten plus years later, it seems every restaurant I pass has something sweet potato on the menu and research journals are brimming with studies firmly establishing the nutritional value of the most versatile vegetable I know. More importantly, a new level of attention is being given to the importance of plant based eating in preventing disease and supporting graceful aging.

Rita Elkins said, in her 1999 publication Wild Yams, "The simple truth is that our twentieth-century lifestyle creates a great deal of health risks not previously experienced by earlier generations." [7] It seems we still have a lot of work to do in the 21st century.

I know you still will want to enjoy mama's and grandma's sweet potato dishes and holiday delights. But you now know there is a wonderful, delicious fascinating world for the sweet potato lover that goes Beyond Candies Yams and Sweet Potato Pie!

ENDNOTES

1. Louisiana Agricultural Experiment Station (Edited by A. Jones and J. C. Bouwkamp. Fifty Years of Cooperative Sweetpotato Research. (Louisiana State University, Louisiana), iii
2. George Washington Carver Agricultural Experiment Station (Edited by Dr. Ralphenia Pace, Dr. Eunice Bonsi, Dr. John Lu). Sweet Potato: Recipes and Nutritional Information. (Tuskegee University, Alabama), 2
3. http://macrobiotics.co.uk/sugar.htm
4. http://www.sucrose.com/bonechar.html
5. Deis, R. C. (2001) - Sweeteners for Health Foods www.foodproductdesign.com/archive/2001/0201ap.html
6. http://www.fitsugar.com/Got-Seasonal-Allergies-Eat-Local-Honey-258237 (retrieved 1-20-12)
7. http://www.webmd.com/vitamins-supplements/ingredientmono-682-STEVIA.aspx?activeIngredientId=682&activeIngredientName=STEVIA
8. http://www.living-foods.com/articles/enzymes.html (retrieved 1-20-12)
9. Rita Elkins, M.H. Wild Yam:Nature's Progesterone (Woodland Publishing, Utah, 1999), 7

INDEX

A
- Avocado key lime pie,

Awesome Rawsome

B
- Biscuits,
- Broccoli portabella bake w/sweet potato crust
- Brownies – sweet potato
- Brown rice veggie casserole,
- Butternut squash soup,

C
- Carrot cake w/cream cheese icing,
- Cherry-tater salad,
- Cheesecake – sweet potato,
- Cobbler – sweet potato,
- Coleslaw,
- Cookies – sweet potato,
- Cranberry sweet potato cake w/rum butter cream icing,
- Cupcakes – sweet potato,

E

Entrees & Sides

G
- Grilled sweet potatoes,
- Ground cherry salsa,

H

How Sweet it is

I

Introducing Sweet P

J
- Jamaican potato pudding cake,

K
- Key lime pie,

N
- Navy bean soup,
- Navy bean squash soup,
- No bake cookies,

P
- Pancakes,

Plant based eating made easy,

- Pound cake – sweet potato,
- Pudding – sweet,

R
- Rawsome sweet potato cheesecake,
- Red pepper & sweet potato pasta,
- Red russet sweet potato soup,
- Roasted rosemary sweet potato wedges,

S
- Scalloped sweet potatoes,

Soups & Salads,
- Spiced sweet potato soup,
- Stove top roasted sweet potatoes,
- Sweet n' sour slaw,
- Sweet potato and greens,
- Sweet potato brownies,
- Sweet potato cheesecake,
- Sweet potato chili,
- Sweet potato cookies,
- Sweet potato cupcakes,
- Sweet potato corn soup,
- Sweet potato crab cakes,
- Sweet potato fries,
- Sweet potato muffins,
- Sweet potato pancakes,

- Sweet potato pound cake,
- Sweet potato pudding,
- Sweet potato quiche,
- Sweet potato salad,
- Sweet potato zucchini bake,

T
- Tempeh; cooking with,
- Tempeh pasta salad,

V
- Vegetable chili,
- Vegetable sweet potato pancakes,

W

Y
- Yam dip,

ABOUT THE AUTHOR

Dr. Velonda Thompson is a health promotion educator specializing in nutrition coaching and meal makeover workshops and seminars. In 1979, as an entrepreneur, she founded Be-Fit, Inc. Dr. Velonda and her team of fitness professionals provided fitness direction for corporate, small businesses. Client list includes New Center Community Services, Blue Care Network, Detroit Public Library, Detroit Area Agency on Aging and AARP. She currently holds an executive position with the Detroit, Michigan Institute for Population Health as Women, Infant and Children (WIC) program manager and Breastfeeding Coordinator.

Ms. Thompson has completed doctoral studies in the field of nutrition and health promotion and is currently a nutrition Professor for South University Online. As a nutritionist, Dr. Thompson is the author of an educational cookbook entitled "Pass the Sweet Potatoes, Please!" As a researcher and lecturer she is a regular conference presenter and keynote speaker both locally and nationally. Dr. Thompson has explored organic farming and nutrition in Ghana, West Africa. Dr. Thompson has also spent numerous years in the non-profit sector facilitating physical fitness, nutrition education and health promotion activities for youth 6 years of age and older. She is also the author of "Calm under Fire", a motivational resource discussing the power of positive self-talk and is now penning her first children's educational cookbook.

View, subscribe, like and follow Dr. Velonda's Nutrition Nuggets:
    BLOG: http://drvelonda.blogspot.com
    TWITTER: #drvelonda
    FACEBOOK: Be-fit, Inc or Velonda Thompson
    EMAIL: drvelonda@gmail.com

Made in the USA
San Bernardino, CA
07 November 2014